3º DAYS TO A SEXIER YOU

by
Paula Peisner Coxe
and
Jessica Daniels

Sourcebooks
Inc.

Naperville, IL

Published by: **Sourcebooks, Inc.**
P.O. Box 372
Naperville, Illinois, 60566
(708) 961-3900
FAX: 708-961-2168

Cover Design: Wayne Johnson
Interior Design and Production: Andrew Sardina
Illustrations by: Jessica Daniels
Additional Illustrations by: Andrew Sardina, Sourcebooks, Inc.
    for the following pages: 9, 11, 15, 16, 21, 29, 31, 34, 37, 44,
    48, 57, 63, 64, 71, 74, 80, 83, 85, 87, 99, 102, 105, 107

Library of Congress Cataloging-in-Publication Data

Peisner Coxe, Paula
        30 days to a sexier you / Paula Peisner Coxe and
    Jessica Daniels.
            p.   cm.
        ISBN 1-57071-054-6 (pbk.) : $6.95.
            1. Women—Sexual behavior.   2. Sexual attraction.
        3. Sex (Psychology)   4. Self-help techniques.   I. Daniels,
        Jessica.   II. Title.
        HQ29.P43   1995
        646.7'0082 — dc20   95-23995
                                                            CIP

Printed and bound in the United States of America.

Paperback — 10 9 8 7 6 5 4 3 2 1

**I don't want to make money.
I just want to be wonderful.**

—Marilyn Monroe

DEDICATION

**To Sharing Our Uniqueness
And Beauty With The World**

CONTENTS

Week 2

Week 3

Week 4

INTRODUCTION

Let's face it girls. Sexy is better. Sexy is better than not sexy...much better. Like many of us, you may think sexy is an hourglass figure, long shiny hair, fresh dewy skin and a full, luscious mouth. We can't lie. That's part of sexy, but just the window dressing. We're here to tell you sexy is an attitude...and you can have it too!

Yes, sexy is an attitude. Sexy is a state of mind. It's the way you walk, your smile, the glint in your eyes, the way you turn your head and roll your fingers through your hair. It's how you feel about yourself and how you feel about life. It's confidence. It's saying, "I feel good about myself and I'm someone darn special."

How many gorgeous women have you seen who walk with a slouch, chew on their hair as they twirl it or speak in a mumbled voice? These unfortunate females lack the self-confidence of a truly sexy person. They're too absorbed in their own world to be aware of others. This surely is not appealing.

Now don't get us wrong. It helps to have a body like Cindy Crawford, but how many of us are that lucky? Apart from genetics, there's only so much you can do to attain that state of perfection.

However, we are talking about REAL LIFE...not perfection. In fact, sexy is imperfect. Sexy is ageless. It's the crinkle around your eyes, showing the woman of experience that you are. It's the quirky smile that's a bit lopsided and, yet, inviting.

For the women in the world who, like us, have a wrinkle here and a love handle there, we have pulled together a 30 Day Attitude Adjustment Plan, one sure to make you feel sexy and have fun getting there. This is not a book on exercise, diet or grooming. It is a book about the real you inside. Like a flower ready to bloom, you have the power to unleash the temptress within yourself.

We have designed a four week plan to ignite the fire burning inside you, to bring out the uninhibited, SEXY you.

Week One—Love Your Body: This week will focus on feeling good about yourself and loving yourself, whether you are fat or thin, short or tall.

Week Two—The Sensual You: This chapter is designed to heighten your sense of touch, smell, taste, hearing and sight.

Week Three—Your Mind: This section is designed to stimulate your ability to rest, calm yourself, find serenity and be at ease.

Week Four—The Creative You: This week we'll look into ways to let out your imagination and expand the way you see the world and others. We'll tempt your fantasies.

Choose any activity in the week. Select what feels comfortable to you. Not all suggestions will fit everyone, so adapt what we've offered to your own lifestyle. We would prefer you look at this book as a menu of desserts. Pick and choose, sample the ones that work for you, the ones that you find nourishing to your spirit and your soul. The wide array of activities in the 30 days are designed to bring out the best in you, to bring out the sexy you. We have intentionally strived for activities that don't cost much. Sexy is not expensive. Sexy is smart.

So, with this in mind, let's begin. Turn the page and hurry down the wondrous path to the beauty that lies within, to all that is you.

Week 1
LOVE YOUR BODY

First, let's take a self-inventory. We are not talking about pounds or muscle tone. Take a good look at yourself, all alone. In the privacy of your home, go to a bathroom or your bedroom where you have a mirror. Look yourself in the eye and assess what you want. What results do you expect? What is sexy to you? What do you need to do to get there? Be kind to yourself. You are your own best friend. Believe that you can be all that you want to be. You can concentrate on any body part—any part of you.

Let's begin with a smile. Smile into the mirror. A smile is what everyone sees first. A good man would walk a mile for a sexy smile. How is your smile? Does it come easily for you? Do you smile often? Look into your eyes. Do they talk? Is there a sparkle? Get a fashion magazine or find a picture you like. Hold the photo next to your face and look in the mirror. Smile. What does the model have that you don't...Probably nothing. She's getting paid to look good. Look at yourself again. Think of a sweet memory...puppies... Christmas...getting that big raise...or better yet, winning the lottery. Watch your smile change. Your face muscles soften. Your face flushes. Your breathing quickens. Your eyes get bigger. Look at yourself. Look at that sexy smile. Remember the Mona Lisa? Men have been mooning over that smile for years. She is a fat lady with straight hair and no eyebrows—but what a smile! People think, "What is she thinking? Wow, is she interesting—I'd like to know *her*!" Her smile is inviting. Practice. You are interesting. You are worth knowing. You are inviting.

Love sonnets have been written about pearly white teeth since the beginning of time. When was the last time you went to the dentist? Are your teeth clean? Sweet smelling breath and teeth like pearls. What a combination! Smiling is the single most important way to communicate. It is even more expressive than words. Your smile makes you pretty special.

OK. Now, take a look at the rest of you. Do you have smooth, sweet smelling skin? We are not talking about lumps and bumps. Everyone has lumps and bumps...even your mate. Are your knees smooth? Are your elbows smooth? How about your heels and

6

ankles? Feet are part of the sexiest you! Look at all those little dimples. We all have them. Men love dimples. Dimples are soft. Dimples make us smile. Remember that we are working on the entire you, not separate pieces of you. Don't get hung up on, "if only I could lose those ten pounds...if only my hair were longer...if only...if only..." Relax. This is your body.

Your body deserves to be loved by you. It's soft and pretty and round. Feel yourself all over. Get some cream and slather it everywhere. Find all those little nooks and crannies you take for granted. Say "hello" to yourself. It's adventure time and you are the star.

Congratulations! You have taken inventory of your beautiful self. You now know where you are, and where you want to be. Now, let's find out what you need to do to get there.

GIVE YOURSELF
A LITTLE PRESENT

Use your own guest soap. Treat yourself to the guest soap that you normally reserve for special occasions. Guest soap is for someone special. You are special. You're the most special person in the world. Find that little antique dish you have been saving. Place it next to your sink. Put in those roses or stars or shell soap. Use one every day this month.

OIL YOUR
SKIN

Soft skin feels good. Baby soft skin feels sexy. Our skin reflects how we are treating our bodies. Our skin needs plenty of nutrients to become more soft and supple to the touch. Skin is forever exposed to the elements: sun, wind, water and cold weather. Over the years, it needs to rehydrate, to rejuvenate and rebuild. Start nurturing your skin today with sweet baby oil. After your shower or bath, generously spread the oil all over your body, your feet, legs, buns, tummy, chest, shoulders, neck and arms. Let your hands slowly apply the oil. There's no rush. Be proud of your fragrant, soft skin. Take a little time to be good to yourself. Pat yourself dry slowly. Think pleasant thoughts.

SPRITZ PERFUME ON YOUR FEET

Imagine being holed up in high heels all day. After wearing high heels and standing a good part of the day, your feet need a break.

Be good to them and to your nose. Spritz your favorite perfume on your feet before you slip on your stockings. Your feet will thank you and so will your shoes. Don't stop here. This works even better with running shoes. Your feet will never be the same. We want happy, sexy toes and feet.

11

SLEEP
A LOT

After a great night's sleep, we feel renewed. Through sleep, we are able to recharge and rest our body and mind. We feel better, look fresher and have more energy. Feeling sexy requires lots of sleep to give us a boost.

GET A FACIAL

Allow yourself to be pampered. A good facial is more than worth the effort. It is cleansing, invigorating and beautifying. A facialist can massage your skin, scrub it, steam it and cleanse every pore. You'll leave the salon with the freshly scrubbed shine of a teenager, soft and clean. There are many different types of facials. Be sure to ask around to find the one that fits your needs.

13

HAVE YOUR
MAKEUP DONE

A new you. Give yourself the works! Red lipstick or will it be earth tones today? Have a professional makeup artist use your face as a pallete. Consider yourself a fine work of art. Allow yourself to take on a new look with each brush stroke. Dare to be different. Often there are makeup artists in department stores who will apply their cosmetics line on you at no cost in order to persuade you to make a purchase. You can also go to a private salon for the pampering. Some salons and department stores have computer imaging. Your makeup can be applied to your picture while you watch. Whatever you decide, open your mind to the possibilities. You're worth it!

WEAR BLACK
LINGERIE

Nothing makes you feel sexier than black lingerie. If you have not yet stocked your wardrobe with black lingerie, you must go out and buy something at once. Purchase the sexiest bra and panties or the most revealing teddy you can find. Go home and put it on!

Garter belts are wonderful and very comfortable. Try the lace top black stockings. Let the allure of the black lace show through your light-colored blouse. The hint of the outline stirs the imagination of your admirer. Often what we imagine is more tantalizing than what we can see.

GET A NEW HAIRSTYLE

Sweet smelling, silky hair is very sexy. How long have you had the same hairstyle? Probably, too long. It's safe and comfortable when things stay the same. It's also boring. If you're like most of us, you can probably blow dry your hair with your eyes closed. Boring isn't sexy. Movement and energy is sexy. You may want to look through some magazines to get an idea of what you'd like. What's new? Consider a subtle change of color, or maybe now is the right time for a big change. Adjust some highlights to bring out the blonde. Soften the grey or deepen the brunette. Look at the length of your hair, its shape, color, shine and body. Does it say, "I'm healthy. I'm alive"? That's the sexy way to wear your hair. It moves as you walk. It's touchable.

TAKE A FAST WALK

Walking is one of the most enjoyable forms of exercise and one that most all of us can do. It strengthens your heart and builds new energy. And energy is sexy! You don't need to belong to a gym. It's better to have the weather on your side. Exercise is a wonderful way to be good to yourself. It's most important to wear the right shoes and put on a new attitude. See yourself building up to a fast pace at greater lengths. And enjoy! You're doing this for you. Remember that as you take each step, you are nearing the energy, spirit and vitality within.

MAKE A
HEALTHY DESSERT

A fresh fruit salad. Raspberry sorbet. Angel food cake. These are a few of the low-fat, low-sugar desserts that taste sexy and are good for you. Eating the right things doesn't have to be boring. Ignite that old sweet tooth and splurge with something good for your body and your spirit. You deserve a treat that's good for you because you are good to yourself.

DRINK LOTS OF WATER

Water purifies and cleanses. It is one of the best foods for the body and enables us to improve our digestion, as well as the softness of our skin. By drinking lots of water, we often feel less hungry as well.

When you long for a carbonated soda or a cup of coffee, reach for a fresh glass of water instead. We all spend so much time in our cars, so why not keep a bottle of water there to drink on our drive to and from work. It is said that eight glasses of water a day is a good for you. You really can't drink too much. You'll feel great and look good too!

19

BUY AN EXERCISE VIDEO AND DO IT

Sweating can be sexy. You can sweat to the oldies, the hardbodies or the stair climbers. Whatever your preference, Richard Simmons, Jane or Buns of Steel, you can do something good for yourself by spending twenty to thirty minutes only two or three times a week to jump, sweat, stretch and use those wonderful muscles of yours.

There's no need to push it. Start off slow and gradually build to a workout. Do what feels comfortable. You can gain without pain. Exercising can be fun with the right attitude. With a slight attitude adjustment and a fitter body, you will feel and look sexier and younger. There's no secret, just hard work.

TAKE A WEIGHTLIFTING CLASS

Imagine the feel of strong, hard biceps, firm buns and a washboard stomach. Hard is sexy. Now, maybe it is an uphill battle to have a body like Cindy, but there's no reason why we all can't climb the hill step by step to tone up and firm up. Even if you are thin, you may benefit from toning. Weightlifting lets you use the muscles that you have. It's exhilarating to feel muscles you thought you had lost or maybe never knew you had. With a toner body, you'll surely feel more comfortable wearing those tight pants or that short skirt. You are the artist and your body is the clay. Sculpt it to your heart's content.

21

FAST FOR
A DAY

Purging your system of impurities makes room for a fresh start and renewed vigor. Allowing your body only liquids for a day allows you the opportunity to cleanse, purify and release the toxins that have built up over time. Invite in the new and release the old.

LAUGH A LOT TODAY

Laughing is one of the healthiest things we can do for ourselves. Laughing from the bottom of our belly, bringing ourselves to tears, leaves us exhausted with joy. The emotions and sense of relaxation it leaves us with is intoxicating. Laugh a lot today. Find humor and joy in simple things. Learn a new joke. Tell a friend. Share your laughter.

WEAR A
LITTLE HELP

We all have a bump or a bulge here or there. If you want to flatten that tummy or push up those breasts, enlist some help. The lingerie department of your neighborhood store is replete with items to fix what mother nature has bestowed on us. Why not? No one will know. As we know ladies, the shapely figure of many a bride is assisted with the support of the widow's girdle to create the perfect hourglass figure. From brides to matrons, women possess many secrets and that's great. Push it up. Press it in. Do whatever makes you feel good and enlist the support of any cloth-covered friend.

Week 2
THE SENSUAL YOU

The taste of warm raspberries melting over a rich, french vanilla ice cream served in a crystal dish...the smell of jasmine in the night air...the sight of a sunset over the ocean on a balmy summer night...the sound of a sultry saxophone singing a sweet lullaby...the touch of a soft, cashmere sweater that hugs you close. These senses make up an important part of you. Too often we forget to stop and smell the roses. This week your goal is to awaken those senses that make you feel sexy, that make you smell the sweetness, hear the melody, feel the warmth, see the beauty and touch the softness.

Some people are more visual. They like looking through their eyes at the visual tapestry of life, at colors, at beauty, at light and shape. Others prefer to live through their auditory senses. The sound of a haunting melody or the whisper of a deep, husky voice are music to many a woman's soul. Whatever stirs your passions, whatever your sense of preference, embrace it and unleash it. Try any or all of the activities in this week and repeat the ones you like best. They are categorized by the predominant sensory area stimulated: sight, sound, taste, touch, smell and feeling. While an activity may impact several sensory areas, the activity is categorized by the major sense affected.

Find a comfortable chair and close your eyes. Imagine lying on freshly mowed grass...spread-eagle. Breathe deeply. The smell is so sweet you can't get enough of it. You push your fingertips deep into the thick carpet. You feel the grass tickle the soles of your feet as you wiggle your toes deeper into its lushness. The fragrance is intoxicating as you roll onto your tummy and bury your face in the scent. Morning dew brushes your cheeks and you pluck a few blades of grass to examine them up close. So small, yet so beautiful. There are dozens of shades of green...blue green at the base with a hint of lavender...deeper kelly green with a golden tinge...feathery yellow at the edges. The more you look, the more colors you find. You turn them round and round examining them, and just before you release them to the wind, you carefully place them into your mouth between your teeth and take a bite. Taste the quick sensation of tartness as the juice attacks your tastebuds. Roll over onto your back again and breathe deeply... from your toes. Surely you don't want to leave and you don't really have to.

Wake up those senses! Little friends awaken! Touch. Smell. Taste. Feel. Hear. They belong to you. Discover yourself and your senses together. Heighten your awareness and nurture your inner beauty. Soon you will begin to share your newest sensations with a special person.

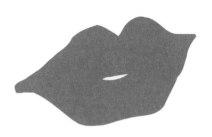

WEAR AN EXCITING COLOR

Never underestimate the power of color. Feeling tired? Feeling blue? Wear Day-Glo socks for a day and see how much more energy you suddenly have. Is life too hectic lately? Do you want to feel virginal again? Dress all in white today. All in white...from the inside out...panties and everything. Want more power and confidence? Wear candy apple red...maybe in a red silk blouse.

What comes to mind when you think about a bold summer yellow...deep, rich royal blue...or sizzling hot pink? We don't have to tell you how naughty black makes us feel. Wonderful, diaphanous black bras, stockings and panties make all of us feel like bad girls.

Colors make a statement. They say, "I'm sure of myself. I'm living life. Look at me!" Whatever color you find exciting or uplifting, wear it. It will be sure to brighten your spirits and add a gait to your walk. Remember, color has movement and it can move you and your mate. That's sexy!

29

Week 2:
THE SENSUAL YOU—Sight

WALK AROUND YOUR NEIGHBORHOOD AND NOTICE TEN THINGS OF BEAUTY

Like many of us, you are probably a creature of habit. Driving down the same road on the same day at the same time, much of the beauty around us is missed as we go through the motions. Our mind wanders as we plan the next move. There are many things of beauty around us, yet we are too busy and too preoccupied to appreciate them. More likely than not, beauty is found in the little things...in the flower that makes its way through the fence to find the sunlight...the giggling toddlers laughing and playing in their front yard...the old storefront preserved in its simplicity...and the smile of the neighborhood store clerk. Beauty is all around us. It comes in all shapes and sizes. It is up to us to seek it out and appreciate it in all its splendor.

Week 2:
THE SENSUAL YOU—Sight

TAKE A WALK WITH NATURE

The beauty of spring flowers, a winter's first snow, the crashing waves of the ocean, the still of the lake, the scents of the forest. Nature's splendor is in our backyard. We need only open our eyes to enjoy it. No matter where we live, there is wonder.

In the quiet of a nature walk, all the colors, scents and images overwhelm the senses. Thinking becomes clearer. The air is crisper and breathing is a pleasure. To appreciate the greenness of the grass, the height of the trees and the color of a freshly-bloomed flower is to appreciate living. Be aware of the beauty around us and the beauty that is you.

GO TO A DEPARTMENT STORE AND BUY PUSH-UP BRAS

Cleavage is sexy. Marilyn had it and so can you. What God did not bestow, we can create through the magic of illusion. Don't worry if you think you're saggy, big, small or in between. Sashay right into your nearest lingerie department and pick out the sexiest, laciest and blackest push up bra. Go home in it. No one will know but you until you drape yourself in your lowest cut evening dress, your sheerest blouse or your funkiest white t-shirt. Then all eyes will be on you as your admirers wonder about the beauty that lurks beneath.

BUY YOURSELF SHOCKING PINK NAIL POLISH

Pretty in pink. That's us girls. We're feminine, alive and want to show it. Even if it's winter with five feet of snow on the ground, lacquer on a new shade of the brightest, most beguiling shade of hot, sizzling pink polish. If your nails are short, that's okay. Why not go out and have some nails put on that are long? Paint your toenails. As you run your hands down the back of your favorite man, imagine him squealing with delight at the touch of you.

EAT DINNER TONIGHT WITH CANDLES AND MUSIC

Turn off your mind and turn on the music. No matter what you're having for dinner tonight...Lean Cuisine or steak tartar...set the stage for a romantic dinner with yourself. You are a wonderful companion. Use your best linen, crystal and china. Light the candles. Turn on the stereo to something soothing and relaxing. Listen to the music. Taste each flavor as you take your time. Relax between bites. Think about the most romantic times in your life, when you felt uninhibited, alive and sexy. What was it that made it so good for you? What can you do today to bring that back? Let the music whisper the answers.

SIT IN THE PARK AND COUNT THE SOUNDS AROUND YOU

Find a bench and close your eyes.

Can you hear the very soft, hushed sounds around you? What are they saying? It's easy to pay attention to the loud, obvious noise we hear, but far more challenging to strain a bit. Reach beyond and hear the important whispers.

Breezes playing with the leaves and grass...birds singing...cats and dogs playing...frogs greeting the lake...crickets announcing their arrival...giggles of little ones...the passion of a young couple...fragments of stories from the old timers...the distant car horn...a ball bouncing. Listen to the soft subtleties of the world around you. The array of all these wonderful sounds and more are the very fabric of life. See how many sounds you are able to distinguish.

TAPE YOUR VOICE AND PLAY IT BACK

How do you sound? Is your voice harried...nervous...high-pitched...
whining...nasal? Do you sound happy...soft spoken...well-modulat-
ed? Listen. Are you husky and throaty...clear and caressing? Listen
again. Strive for a pleasing sound. Tape your voice at different times
of the day and night. Compare your voice tape to your TV heroine.
Do you hear a sultry, soothing, soft you? You can adjust your voice
to the situation. Try a firm, professional sound, then a soft, understanding tone. The voice is very seductive. Be open-minded.
Observe your intonation, pitch, and especially your volume.
Remember, your voice is ageless and it presents your message like
a beautifully wrapped gift. What are you intending to say?

GET A FAVORITE PIECE OF MUSIC TO DANCE TO ALONE

Romance. Getting in the mood. What better way than to be serenaded by your favorite guitar, bass, violin or cello? Make your kitchen a chandelier-draped ballroom, your living room a candlelit club. Turn the lights down low and become your own Fred and Ginger all rolled into one. As you take each step, feel the music transport you to another time, another place. You are at the center of the dance floor. All eyes are on you. Create the moment.

BUY A
NEW PERFUME

How long have you been wearing the same fragrance? ...That long, huh? Well, it's time for a change. Break out of your old mold. Go for a completely new scent.

Shop the department store perfume counters. The selections will delight you. You will have a wonderful time. Spritz away! Buy sample sizes. If you don't like one, try another. Experiment. Have fun. If you tend towards musk, try a floral scent. If you like a heavy fragrance, buy a light and airy perfume. Spray behind your ears, on your wrists and behind your knees. Lavish your body in a new aroma… lavender…rose…heliotrope… jasmine…sweet smelling… ambrosial…fruity. Buy an atomizer, scent bottle, scent bag, sachet or pomander. Let your body say, "I'm ready for some excitement!"

SPRAY PERFUME IN YOUR UNDERWEAR DRAWER

Why not spray some luscious perfume on those pieces of lace and cotton that we keep close to our most intimate parts? Lightly spray perfume in your underwear drawer. As you open the drawer each morning you will be pleasantly greeted with a blush of jasmine, musk or rose scent. Say "hello" to a sweeter day and a lovelier you.

PUT POTPOURRI IN YOUR FAVORITE PLACES

Rich botanical and essential oils, flower petals and lovely scents, potpourri can create a soothing and inviting aroma throughout your home. Place some in a little dish in any room. You can even create a rainbow of colors with an assortment of different potpourri. Put some in your finest crystal dish and set it in one of your favorite places. Make sure you spend a few minutes sitting nearby each day.

MAKE YOUR HOME SMELL LIKE FRESH BAKED MUFFINS

Take a small saucepan. Add about one and one-half cups of water, break 2-3 cinnamon sticks into it, some cloves, a pinch of allspice, and some slices of lemons and oranges. Simmer for about 10 minutes. Do not boil. Turn the heat off. Leave the saucepan on the stove for awhile.

It will smell like you've been baking for days. The aroma takes you back to childhood and holidays—cozy and warm and friendly. It makes the entire house smell like home-baked muffins and cakes.

You can feel very accomplished with this little scent. It can fill up a lonely house and keep you company while you read the paper or watch the news, or brew some up before your date arrives. We all know how our men love their cakes and muffins. He will certainly want to come back to your house. Food can be sexy, but this is not fattening! Take a deep breath of the fresh scent.

41

NIBBLE AT A PIECE OF CHOCOLATE FOR THIRTY MINUTES

Chocoholics unite! Now you can indulge for the good of your spirit. Don't worry about the calories for one day. Take a few pieces of your favorite chocolate. Select a comfortable place to lounge and nibble at the sexiest of all foods. Savor the scent of each morsel. Rub the richness across your lips. Slowly place it in your mouth. Slide your tongue over the texture. Make it melt in your mouth until your tastebuds scream. Swallow slowly in small amounts. Taste again as it glides down your throat. A good piece of chocolate, slowly savored, is a sexy way to say hello to ourselves. Think how much fun it could be for two people to enjoy the same piece of chocolate.

INDULGE YOURSELF WITH A BOTTLE OF YOUR FAVORITE CHAMPAGNE

A bubbly bottle of your favorite champagne is the perfect elixir. Open the china closet and get a champagne glass. Buy a split. It's the perfect size for a glass and a half. Enjoy a glass while taking a bubble bath or while sitting by the fire. Add some sparkle to your routine. Why not drink a glass at the kitchen table while doing your bills or opening your mail? Champagne adds a bit of flair to the ordinary. Celebrate the sensation as each bubble kisses your lips.

MAKE A SUCKER LAST IN YOUR MOUTH WITHOUT BITING IT

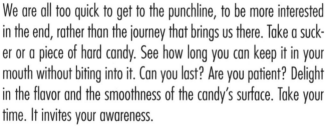

We are all too quick to get to the punchline, to be more interested in the end, rather than the journey that brings us there. Take a sucker or a piece of hard candy. See how long you can keep it in your mouth without biting into it. Can you last? Are you patient? Delight in the flavor and the smoothness of the candy's surface. Take your time. It invites your awareness.

SLOWLY SAVOR A RICH ICE CREAM DESSERT

(Don't despair here ladies, fat-free yogurt works the same)

Since the time we were children to the moment our adult cravings were cast, nothing, but nothing, seems more soothing than a great dish of ice cream. In a cone or a cup, plain or smothered in hot fudge, this is an aphrodisiac. It's sexy. It's a great exercise for your lips and mouth. Eat it slowly. With each lick of your tongue, pretend it is the last scoop in the world. Make it last. Just as the last melting drop escapes and drips down your chin, lick it up with your tongue. Like a good man, don't let it get away.

WEAR A
SILK BLOUSE

Silk, softly caressing your shoulders, draped across your chest is one of the sexiest materials to the touch. The whisper softness of the fabric allows it to breathe. It can be warm and cradle your curves, or cold and make your skin's surface tingle. Silk says sexy and it is feminine and alluring. It says, "I want to touch and to be touched."

GET A FULL BODY MASSAGE

Stiff neck? Lower back pain? Sore shoulders? Aching feet? These are all normal symptoms of our daily life. We live in a speeded-up world...computers...fax machines...portable phones. We try to do too much. We try to satisfy everyone. Today it's your turn to satisfy yourself.

How many times have you heard that your body is your temple? Treat your body with respect and it will return the favor a hundredfold. A full body massage will allow you to release the tension built up in your neck, shoulders and back. It's amazing how much tension we keep in our hands and in our feet. Massaging the deep tissue is purifying. Relax and let yourself go. You deserve to be pampered, to be touched, to feel good.

GIVE YOURSELF
A FOOT
MASSAGE

Nothing is as wonderful as having someone take your foot in their two hands while they caress each toe, then helplessly watching as a kiss is planted inside your instep. The feet are one of the most sensual parts of the body. Get to know your feet. If you don't know how to start your massage, sit on the edge of your bathtub and put your feet under the water spout. Adjust the temperature and water force to "medium" and feel the tingle as your blood starts to circulate. It feels like heaven must be. Take out your body cream and enjoy. Definitely use your fluffy bath towels for yourself. Our feet have the power to relax other parts of our body like our neck and back. Practice on yourself, then do this massage to your partner.

TAKE A
BUBBLE BATH

Indulgence. Surround yourself with clouds of scented bubbles. Soft, warm water, caressing your skin...for you alone. Stay in the tub as long as you want. Read a good book. Meditate. Think about your dreams. Take a bath by candlelight with a nice glass of wine and classical music serenading you. Later you may want to add a partner.

PLANT SOME FLOWERS

Dig in the yard. Kneading, sifting the raw earth through your fingers, your hands create life from a seed. Apartment bound? Buy a clay pot or get a window box.

The feel of the moist soil against your palms brings back memories of childhood, of molding clay and playing in the dirt. As you build your garden of lilies, lilacs, roses or any flower you choose, find comfort in your garden. You are responsible for giving it life and keeping it alive. The drops of water you pour on each petal, the kindness with which you clip the branches, and the time you take to nourish the soil are all gifts of life. Your hands reach out to nature.

TOUCH
MORE TODAY

Touching can bring forth a myriad of emotions. Warmth. Sensuality. Comfort. Acceptance. There are many simple ways we can touch more often. A simple pat on the back. A hug. A handshake. Reaching out to touch someone's arm or hand as we tell them something brings forth sincerity and interest. A touch says a lot. It is a way of reaching out and making someone feel good, and you feel good while doing it.

HUG A
LOT TODAY

A warm, strong embrace is soothing. Wrapping your arms around someone in a slow and sensual way is inviting. Placing your hands in certain spots is alluring. A hug says a lot. Touching and caressing another person brings you nearer to them and to yourself. Be generous with your hugs. There is an infinite amount to go around.

TAKE
THE PLUNGE

Go for a relaxing swim. Get into a virtual weightless state in a large body of water. Go farther and faster. The backhand. The butterfly. The breast stroke. Take a kickboard and push yourself along...keep moving. Feel each muscle as it is stretched, propelling you through the water. You are one with the water, cutting a razor-like path to and from each side of the pool. With each stroke, with each movement of a tired muscle, you become stronger, more refreshed and ready for a new day. No pool? Get to the beach, pond or lake. Squish sand through those toes. Power walk in the water. Enjoy yourself. Water is soothing, energizing and therapeutic. Water symbolizes rebirth. Please, don't get stuck in the bathing suit rut. Put your suit on no matter what you think it looks like on you. Just get out and do it. Let's get some energy. Energy is sexy.

SPLASH

53

DO HOUSEWORK IN THE NUDE WITH HIGH HEELS

Pull the shades down and close the blinds. Crank up the stereo and you're ready to get out the cleaning supplies. Skip the bathrooms and the kitchen. It's dust and polish time. Cleaning will never be the same again. As you polish that piece of fine wood furniture, imagine you're applying body oil to your favorite man. Take your time. The oil seeps into his pores with each stroke of your hand. Make designs...see how playful your fingers can be. Imagine doing a sultry dance with your mate as you push the vacuum along. With each step, with each thrust of your forearms, beckon him to you. Pretend the vacuum hose is the train of your chiffon gown. Make each cleaning activity an exercise in expression, of your body, your sensuality. You can be a burlesque star or Scarlett O'Hara. As you pass in front of the mirrors in your home, take a long, loving look at yourself. Smile. Pose. Play. Enjoy your body and all that is you.

GIVE YOUR OLD CLOTHES TO SOMEONE NEEDY

It doesn't have to be spring to get out with the old and to bring in the new. No matter the time of year, you can always dig into your dressers and closets. Finally take those old pants you wore two years ago and that blouse you love with the tiny stain that's barely visible out of the closet. You know you'll never wear them again. Give them to someone who will appreciate them. What to you is old, stained or the wrong size, may be just perfect for someone who can't afford to buy it. You will feel happy that you have given something to someone in need and have made space in your closet for yourself.

PUT ON YOUR SEXIEST LINGERIE —FOR YOU

Take out that sexy lingerie, the one you bought for that special vacation, for that special evening, or the one you received as a gift, but have yet to wear. Slowly, caressingly, put it on. Savor the femininity, the way it hugs your body, your every curve. Wear it under your sweats, your business attire or whatever you would wear in your daily life. Only you know what is hidden under your jacket, the real woman simmering inside, but I'll bet you act differently today because of your little secret. Enjoy your sexy new feeling.

CALL AN OLD FRIEND YOU HAVEN'T TALKED TO IN A WHILE

There is surely someone in your life who has shared special moments only you two know. And, with time and distance, you have grown apart. Yet, the memories of your time together bring a smile to your face. Making memories is what life is all about. Friends enrich our lives through their support, love, encouragement and kindness. Look into your old phone book to find the special person you lost touch with. Spend some time catching up, remembering the good times or just saying "Hi!—I've been thinking about you." It will seem as though it was yesterday that you were together.

TELL SOMEONE YOU LOVE THEM

The words "I love you" warm the heart and nourish the soul. We often forget to say these three simple words to those we care about the most. Too many times, our minds are racing with worries and preoccupations and we let precious time slip by without saying how we truly feel. You, too, will feel warmth and joy in expressing love. Give and ye shall receive.

Whether it's the man in your life, your child, your parent, your sister or brother, or your friend, everyone wants to be loved. Let them know how you feel. Open your heart.

58

Week 3
YOUR MIND

The possibilities of the universe are at our fingertips. We have only to open our minds. Our minds are our most powerful asset. The mind is capable of creating reality. If we think things are a certain way, more often than not, things turn out just as we imagined. This leads us to the possibility to change the way we view ourselves and the world around us.

Feeling good about yourself is the first step to feeling sexy. It is not an easy task to truly feel good about yourself. We all harbor doubts, anxieties and wishful thoughts about the way things could have been, could be and never will be. Well, ladies, now is as good a time as ever to toss those cares out the window. If life gave you lemons—make lemonade. Even if it is not spring, make up your own spring cleaning with an ATTITUDE ADJUSTMENT. Desire to feel good. You'll be tickled pink with the fruits of your positive mental labor.

Since feeling sexy is a state of mind, as we all know, we have to believe that if the plump lady with the tiny wrinkles walks with a shimmy and a twinkle in her eye, she's got the attitude. She's in a sexy state of mind. To enter this wondrous state, you need a passport to relaxation and serenity.

In a relaxed, serene state, you are open to positive stimulation. Your energy is uplifting and receptive. You think more clearly and act with more purpose. The cloud of worries dissipates in favor of the luxuriating rays of calm and sunshine that reach your spirit and your soul.

You can begin to feel relaxed by recognizing the difference between the relaxed you and the anxious you. How is your voice? Is it high-pitched and sharp or calm and understanding? Do you feel pain in your back and shoulders or are you at rest, barely feeling your toes? Now, think back on your first love, the time you felt the most special. What sensation overcomes you now? Warmth wrapped in a nice smile. The difference is like night and day. While nothing was really changed in your life, you feel different. You have created a different sense of being, simply by using your all-powerful mind.

Fine tune the awareness of your state of being. By concentrating on feeling good, relaxed, at ease and calm, you invite good things into your life. Start feeling sexy by trying on a different attitude. Sexy is not how you look. It's how you feel, and how you feel rests with your mind.

Week three focuses on ways to add more relaxation and serenity into your life. Feeling relaxed and serene evokes a sense of confidence. Confidence is sexy.

Sometimes mindless things are the perfect recipe for relaxation. Spending time doing trivial, mundane things without having to "get things done" can often be relaxing. Take your time wandering through this section. Let your imagination take hold. Serenity awaits.

CREATE THE MOOD

Getting in the mood is a mindset. A surefire way to ignite those sexy feelings is to do sexy things. One night this week when your love is in another room or is coming home at a good hour, leave a trail of your clothes to the bedroom. Or the trail can lead to a luxurious, candlelit bubble bath. Let your love be the explorer and you create the sexy mood. Think provocative, stimulating, inventive thoughts. Your actions will match your thoughts. Sexy is as sexy does.

RECALL YOUR
FIRST LOVE

Our first love holds a special, untouched place in our heart. Find a relaxing spot with no interruptions. Close your eyes and gently walk through the first time love was innocent and your heart filled with desire. Remember the newness of love. The simple passions and the dizzy sensations of pure joy and pain. Young hearts beating faster, aching with shyness and longing. Cherish these memories. Savor the feeling. Your experience with your first love helped form all that you are today.

Week 3:
YOUR MIND

RELAX

When we are in a relaxed state of mind, we release a lot of the tension and stressors from our muscles. The mind is a powerful tool. Its healing powers are infinite. As we learn to relax, our bodies follow. We enjoy more and are open to more. Being open invites good feelings. When we are not relaxed, our mind races in circles with tensions, worries and frustrations. There is no room for loving thoughts. Through relaxation, our bodies can then be satisfied and our mind can envision all that we desire. Relax. Desire. Satisfaction is yours for the taking.

LOOK AT OLD PICTURES AND REMEMBER GOOD TIMES

Good feelings can be found in your photo albums. Relax in one of your favorite chairs, turn off the answering machine, get a cup of tea and slowly thumb through your album. Try to remember how you felt as you look at each picture.

What was the conversation...the laughter...the mood of the moment? Who is in the picture with you? Where are they now? Linger in the feelings that surface as you take a walk down memory lane. What we most remember are the times that create fond memories. Wake up those feelings. Go ahead, create memories today.

READ A FEW CATALOGUES

Catalogues are great places to let your imagination go wild, to find unique and often less expensive items than you may see in the stores. Just peruse the pages and imagine how you would refurnish your home or expand your wardrobe. There are some great gift ideas in those pages. New is sexy. Take a break from the tried and true and imagine exciting ways to decorate your life. You're worth it.

GET THAT DRESS YOU'VE BEEN EYEING

How many times have you seen a great dress and passed it by? Have you even tried it on, only to tell yourself that it wasn't the right time, or you don't need it now or how money can be better spent on other things? Well, now is as good a time as any to give yourself permission to try on that dress and buy it. Charge it if you must. Begin to plan the perfect evening to wear it for the first time. We owe it to ourselves to look and feel our best. Being the best you can be is awfully sexy.

READ A TRASHY BEST-SELLER

Fantasizing is relaxing. Those perfect lovers, bursting with lust and passion. As the pages turn, the touch, the smell of romance becomes more vivid. The characters come alive. It's as though Fabio is in your living room...maybe your bedroom. The passion transcends the pages and the written word becomes reality. You only have to use your imagination.

GO TO A DOUBLE FEATURE

There may still be some around. If you can't find an old-fashioned theater, then a regular matinee will do just fine. Movies are a great escape, and often, fantasizing can make you feel sexy. Sometimes just forgetting about our everyday trials and tribulations is a welcome relief and soothing for the soul. Try escaping to the big screen, to a place larger than life, as the actors play just for you.

READ A
CLASSIC NOVEL

The days of the true gentleman, the fair princess, the romantic novel. The texture of life lies in the classics. Pick up a Hemingway, a Steinbeck or a Stein. The richness of the characters, with words woven to touch our hearts, take us back in time to a place of old when men were men and women were women. As you turn the pages, imagine living in the time, savoring the beauty of all that is life. Relax your mind and escape to a world of old.

TREAT YOURSELF TO SOME FLOWERS

Fresh flowers are inspiring. They bring out the romantic in us. Whether you are passing by a flower shop or feel like having some delivered to your home or office, do it.

Pick the freshest, brightest bouquet you can create. Go for some exotic, long-stemmed flowers like bird-of-paradise. Or a single rose says it all. Wear a gardinia in your lapel. Place your flowers in a special place to remind yourself of the special woman that is you.

ORDER IN
DINNER

The surest path to feeling sexy is to start feeling relaxed. After a long day at the office or running around taking care of the house and the kids, the last thing on your mind is rushing to the kitchen to whip up a gourmet meal. And well it should be the last thing on your mind. You deserve a treat, so why not start today?

Let your fingers do the walking. Select a fabulous neighborhood restaurant. Chinese. Italian. Mexican. Order the works. Even if a pizza place is the only one that delivers, go for it. Now isn't the time to count calories. Count how much energy you've saved by giving yourself the treat of not preparing a meal. The only thing you have to do is make the call and enjoy. Relax for the rest of the evening.

CALL AN OLD BOYFRIEND

Remembering the good times is soothing. Think about that special guy you thought the world of, as he did of you. The times you were in his arms, the warmth of your passion. Then things changed. You went in different directions and met other people. Yet, he still holds a special place in your memories. Without your experience with him, you wouldn't have learned and grown to be the woman that you are today. He helped to create a page in the book of life that is yours.

Call him up. Tell him you were thinking about him. You wanted to say "hi" and hear his voice. Nothing more. Nothing less. Maybe you will both have a few good smiles reminiscing about the old days. Feeling again the excitement and tingle of a woman in love. Being in love with love is sexy.

74

WATCH SOME OLD MOVIES

The romance of an era long lost. *An Affair To Remember. Love Is A Many Splendored Thing. Roman Holiday. Casablanca.* Cary Grant and Deborah Kerr. Bogie and Bacall. Two people as one. A man and a woman. Love. To cherish. To ache. To have your heart break. The tender feelings that can only be evoked by a great old movie. Go to your nearest video store and rent a classic.

Put on your sweats. Make a big bowl of popcorn. Turn off the phone and get comfy on your favorite sofa. Turn the lights down and the movie on. Drift away while your emotions are stirred by the romance of a great love story. The heroine is you. Her love is your special man. Romance is sexy.

TAKE THE
PHONE OFF
THE HOOK

Have you ever just started to doze off in a dreamy, peaceful state when the reverberation of the phone ringing practically caused your toes to curl? The phone has that effect on us at times. It can be our best friend, bringing us good news and cheer, yet it can have the poorest timing and interrupt our most cherished moments.

Start feeling sexy with some quiet time by taking the phone off the hook. Curl up with a good book, meditate or just do nothing. Do whatever makes you feel good. If you want to polish your nails or polish your shoes, you have made time for you. Interruptions aside. The phone off the hook. You are your priority. You are worth it. All else can wait.

TAKE A DRIVE

Imagine the hot summer sun beating on your brow as a cool breeze blows through your hair, driving down the highway in your '68 red, convertible Mustang. Elvis is blasting and you're not looking back. The road ahead beckons. You are in the driver's seat.

Taking a drive can be fun. Just like a teenager, jump in the front seat, pop in your favorite CD or tape, put the petal to the metal and drive to the next adventure.

DO SOME YOGA

There is something sexy in being calm. You can handle anything. You are ready for whatever life has awaiting you. Yoga is the perfect way to center your mind and body and become one. Your breathing will reflect the serenity. Any tension in your muscles will subside.

There may be some classes in the neighborhood or a video tape for beginners. Just try it. If yoga doesn't fascinate you, how about tai chi? It's different and can only add to your knowledge of life and the power of your being.

WRITE LOVE
NOTES TO
YOUR LOVE

Taking the people we love for granted is all too easy. There are never enough hours in the day to show someone how much we care and appreciate them. A great way to start is to write

NOTE INSIDE

it down and say it with spice. Leave your love a note on the bathroom mirror when he is brushing his teeth that says "You are the best and I'll show you how much I appreciate you when you get a chance to meet me in bed...now and not a minute later."

Place a provocative note in his briefcase so he'll thumb through his papers at the office and find your note in red lipstick telling him of all the wonderful things that await him when he gets home. You can be sure he won't be late tonight. You feel naughty just doing it. He feels excited by reading your words. Naughty and excitement are next door neighbors of sexy.

79

KEEP A ROMANTIC REMINDER LIST

We all have our proverbial "to do" lists. Let's add to the usual list of errands and routine-laden chores some exciting, romantic things we must remind ourselves to do every week. Romance is sexy. From buying fresh flowers to sending love notes to planning a night out with your love, you can put romance in your life every day.

Our romantic activities have to be high on the priority list and not relegated to the end of the list or constantly pushed off to the next week. Romance is found in the little things. A little romance every day keeps the homefires burning.

Week 4
THE CREATIVE YOU

This week looks into ways to let out your imagination. We'll expand the way you see the world and others in it. We'll tempt your fantasies. Discovery is exciting. The world offers infinite possibilities to uncover its many beauties.

One of the most exciting ways to feel sexy and to be sexy is to do creative things and get out of our normal, ho-hum routine. Routine is safe and secure, but definitely not sexy. Part of the allure of feeling sexy is the sensations that await you, both that you evoke and that are awakened within you. It is a way of being alive, like how you feel when you take a huge gulp of fresh mountain air on a sunny day.

Sexiness is bringing out the laughter, imagination and spontaneity of youth. It is trying new things, experimenting with the possibilities, finding ways to make lemonade out of lemons, seeing and accepting the good and beauty in all that surrounds us. It is an attitude.

You can create the world around you. You have control over how others treat you and how you are perceived. When you give out positive energy and send your loving thoughts out for the world to receive, the rewards will return tenfold.

Create the state of mind you want by doing new things, trying new attitudes and looking at things in a new light. As though you now have a pair of new glasses with a finer focus on feeling good, feeling sexy, you are able to see the world differently. The woman that you are is wonderful. You possess all the qualities of allure, intrigue and excitement. You are beautiful in mind, body and spirit. Create a wondrous environment to nurture your soul. Let your imagination soar!

TRY A FOREIGN DISH YOU'VE NEVER HAD BEFORE

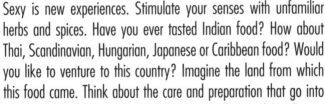

Sexy is new experiences. Stimulate your senses with unfamiliar herbs and spices. Have you ever tasted Indian food? How about Thai, Scandinavian, Hungarian, Japanese or Caribbean food? Would you like to venture to this country? Imagine the land from which this food came. Think about the care and preparation that go into

every spoonful. Observe the table setting. Look at the dishes and silverware. Notice the decor.

As you taste the delicacies, describe the flavors to yourself. Inhale the aromas and critique the texture of the food. Broaden your horizons. Experience the array of richness in life. This is sexy!

83

GIVE SOME OF YOUR TIME TO CHARITY

Giving your time and energy to those who are in need is truly the most generous act we can do. We all write checks and put them in the mail for our favorite charities, but touching someone else with your words or sharing a smile with another will make you feel enriched and satisfied. Even if it is only one or two hours a week, it can make a difference in someone's life. Consider charities for the elderly, for children, for the sick and for the homeless. Reach out and be a part of making the world a better place. Open your heart and give a little of yourself. You will make a difference.

SING YOUR FAVORITE SONGS IN THE SHOWER

Singing makes you feel good. Now you may not be blessed with the vocal chords of a Streisand or a Ronstadt, but who will hear? With the water cascading down your back, and the suds awash in your hair, belt out a few good oldies. Smile as you sing. Put yourself into it. Feel the music.

How about a romantic ballad? If you're in a sultry mood, turn the lights down low, even light some candles and serenade yourself as you lather up. The water drops beating a lusty tune. The steam from the shower creating the mood as you and Billie Holiday start the day.

TAKE PIANO LESSONS

Have you ever imagined being serenaded by your love with the piano as you dined by candlelight in the privacy of your home? Make this fantasy come true. You can learn the piano and make beautiful music together with the one you love. You can create a concerto for one with you as the master. Music is the perfect way to stir the soul.

Week 4:
THE CREATIVE YOU

LEARN A NEW LANGUAGE

Bonjour, madame. Como tallez vous? Ah, que belleza! Usted es una maravilla! Whether in French, Spanish, Italian or any new tongue, the romance and wonder of a new language excites the possibilities. It opens up thoughts of travel, of adventure, of new people. There is so much diversity and color in language. As you learn to say something as simple as hello or goodbye, you open your world to others and to a new part of you. An undiscovered part, an uncharted hideaway where you can use new words to delight, to share your love.

Sexy Sympa Sinlich

Cachondo Cinst cazibe Zmyslowy

Sexig Provocante

87

INVITE YOUR BEST FRIEND ON A PICNIC

Create a marvelous feast of fresh bread, red wine, exotic cheeses and ripe fruit and invite a grand friend on a picnic—on the spur of the moment. Pack your best crystal, napkins, linen and china and spread out under a shady old tree. Why not picnic on the sand, at your favorite beach, at dusk?

The menu, the time and place are up to you. It's sexy to be spontaneous and giving. Combine these traits with good food and friends and you will surely feel abundance and joy. It's sexy to be alive!

WRITE A POEM, SEND A NOTE

A rose is a rose is a rose. Poetry in its simplicity is beautiful. Expressing our emotions through the written word is an art. Bring out the artist inside of you. Think of a pleasant experience, one that brought you warmth, comfort and joy. Now, quickly jot down some words that depict how you feel. Embellish those words with phrases. Tell a little story. Create a picture with words. Now may be the perfect time to express a thank you note or keep-in-touch letter. Don't plan it. Just a few lines is all it takes. Someone will love you for it.

NOTE INSIDE

MAKE A DATE WITH YOURSELF FOR LUNCH

The anticipation of what it will be like, of how you will feel. Remember your first date? The time it took you to get ready, how special you felt. Now is the time to make a first date with you and to pamper yourself because you are interesting, exciting and fun to be with. Make a date with yourself for a fabulous lunch at a wonderful spot. Eat out on the terrace, or at a little table for two. Those tiny tables ensconsced in the corner of the room are not for you. You have reserved the best.

Take your time and slowly review the menu. Enjoy an apéritif or a fresh drink before you are ready to order. Delight in the time you have to relax, sipping your frothy cappuccino and enjoying your own company with no phones ringing and no one tugging at your shoulders. Just a quiet conversation with you is enough. If you prefer to tiptoe and not take the bold step to simply sit at the table alone, bring some reading material. Whatever makes you feel relaxed and at ease. There's something sexy about the solitude and pleasure an attractive woman radiates while confidently dining alone.

SMELL
THE ROSES

In our hurried and run-about world, we feel like we're constantly on the go, hardly having a relaxing moment to eat, steal a nap or read a magazine. Life can seem to hurry along. If life is passing so quickly, what are we doing with it? Smelling the roses goes beyond the literal sense. Surely, when we pass some lovely flowers, we try taking a moment to savor the delicacy of their aroma. However, when there are no flowers around, we can still seize the moment by recognizing and appreciating the many blessings that abound in our world. Linger a moment longer with one task, once a day. Fill your lungs with a big helping of fresh air. Pause. Cherish and embrace the moment.

PLACE YOUR FAVORITE PHOTO IN AN UNUSUALLY DECORATIVE FRAME

Most of us have plain, simple brass, wood or silver-plated picture frames. We cherish the photos of loved ones and of the good times we have had, and yet relegate them to a nondescript, vanilla frame where they are encased for years. Why not visit a flea market, your neighborhood gift store or boutique and get an unusual picture frame?

There are great frames with engravings, bold and pastel colors, lacquered surfaces and jewels. Take the photo with you as you shop around. Pick out a frame that makes a statement. It has character and so do you. Having character is sexy.

WEAR A
BEAUTIFUL SCARF

There are innumerable, marvelous possibilities with scarves. Scarves are the most versatile of accessories and can be used in many ways to accent our wardrobe. Draped around the neck, a scarf can be knotted, bowed or loosely hung. Around our hips, a scarf invites the eye. Placed across our shoulders, a wonderful scarf hints of a continental style, of a feminine appeal.

A bold print, a solid silk or a sheer lace, a scarf can make you feel new and create a whole new look. It is only a small piece of material but has a place in our wardrobe throughout the year, with dresses, pants, coats and jackets. Pull your love close to you with your undraped scarf as you hold him tight in a passionate embrace. Scarves yearn to be touched.

HAVE YOUR COLORS DONE

Colors impact our moods. Wear grey and you feel serious and sullen. Wear white and you feel pure, clean and virginal. Colors influence not only how we feel about ourselves, but cause reactions in others whether they realize it or not. Sometimes we don't even realize the reactions colors cause.

How did you feel the last time you really felt sexy? Now, what were you wearing at the time? What color was it? If a bold red brings out the confidence in you, or a basic black helps you to feel elegant, go with your preferences and wear the colors that you feel best in. More likely than not, these colors will be the ones you look best in also.

When you have your colors done, you will discover whether you are a fall, winter, spring or summer person. The rainbow of colors that are compatible with our skin tone, eyes and coloring offer many possibilities. Like a fine painting where you are the pallete, brush on the colors that create vibrancy and life in your being. You are only limited by your imagination. Let your imagination lead you.

94

PUT CHOCOLATE IN YOUR COFFEE

Adding a touch of sweetness to our coffee or tea makes for a wonderful dessert. Sugar, saccharine and honey are our usual staples and have a place in all of our homes. Why not break the mold and give yourself a delicacy? Chocolate is an aphrodisiac. The texture, taste and aroma of the sweetest of delicacies is sure to satisfy. From a rich, Belgian chocolate to a light, milk chocolate variety, you can add a touch of decadence to your everyday life.

Feeling sexy can often be found in the tingle of something new that livens the senses. A yummy chunk of your favorite chocolate can arouse your tastebuds and leave you wanting more. That feels sexy!

95

PUT DECALS ON YOUR FINGERNAILS

Think about adding a burst of creativity to your regular manicure. Whether you visit a salon or pamper yourself at home, try adding fun decals to the tips of your beautiful fingers. In fact, one inviting decal on just your pinkie may create the flavor you want. As you sip your morning coffee, delight in the design of your chosen decal.

Decals come in all shapes, designs and sizes. One week you may want a lovely red rose, the next week you may feel like a tigress and try a feline character on for size. Whatever strikes you, follow the feeling and get in the mood to be creative, venture out of the box, out of your normal routine and habits. Finding creativity in simple things is exciting. Exciting is sexy.

START A PIGGY BANK FOR AN END-OF-YEAR GIFT FOR YOURSELF

You are worth it. Every time you receive change and find your wallet bulging with unneeded nickles, pennies and change, put them in a piggy bank—a private place for you. As you deposit your coins, imagine the fantastic gift you will give yourself. Jewelry. Clothes. A trip. A massage. There are so many delicious things you can do for yourself. Create fantasies for your favorite gift. Wrap it in a big red bow and give yourself a hug. Be good to yourself and invite others to be good to you too. Feeling good about yourself and deserving of riches is sexy.

MAKE AN EMERGENCY BEAUTY PACK FOR YOUR CAR

The unexpected dinner meeting, the day that goes on longer than planned, or running about for longer than we had thought can leave us a bit unraveled. By keeping an emergency beauty pack in the car, you will have at your fingertips your favorite red lipstick, your powder to sprinkle on any shine, your blush to lift your spirits and any other items you may need. A sure refresher is a cool spritz of perfume to make you feel like you're just getting started. Feeling fresh and energetic is sexy. Anticipate the unexpected and keep a beauty pack around where you most need it.

MAKE A CRAZY THROW CUSHION

Maybe you never thought you could sew or didn't make the time to learn. Well, you don't need to be a master seamstress to create a wonderfully sexy throw cushion for your bed, your sofa or your most comfortable chair. It's all in the material. Pick a sexy color, fabric or design that says, "Touch me...I'm soft, warm and inviting." Maybe it is a rich burgundy, a creme-colored lace or a red velvet that will envelop a fluffy, rich pillow.

You can hand stitch the fabric to the pillow or use your sewing machine. A fabric store will surely have a simple, how-to manual to give you some idea how to get started. Perfection is not the goal. Trying something different is the fun of it. You'll have a sexy, soft ornament waiting for you to arrive, there to caress you.

Week 4:
THE CREATIVE YOU

MAKE A
COLLAGE OF
OLD PHOTOS

Create a collection of your most precious memories by designing a delicious collage of wonderful photos of family, friends and loves. Photos can be framed with dried flowers, drawings, ribbons and jewels to create a potpourri of colors, shapes and images to frame your memories.

Old photos can be like fine paintings that appreciate with time. Delicately treat these memories with care and imaginatively create a display for all to admire. Pick a wonderful frame and hang the finished collage in your dressing area, your bathroom or in a little corner of your bedroom. Reflecting on the past in a warm and loving way will enrich your view of today and all that you are, all that you have and all that you have become.

TREAT YOURSELF TO SOME WILD SUNGLASSES

Mystery can be sexy. What lurks behind those wild sunglasses is yours to know and others to only imagine. Do you have sky blue, alluring eyes, eyes as green as the coral-decorated Caribbean surf or are you a sultry, brown-eyed woman of the world?

Let the imagination soar. Dress your eyes in a wild pair of sexy sunglasses.

The black, retro look invites the imagination. How about a pair encircled with tiny jewels? Envision yourself wearing mirrored lenses that your admirer can see only his reflection in and is left to imagine what lurks behind the lenses. Your neighborhood pharmacy or boutique will have a variety of types, sizes and colors. You need only open your mind to the possibilities. Wear a new attitude when you try on those sexy shades.

GIVE A GIFT TO SOMEONE

Giving lightens the spirit and fills the soul. When we get out of our world of worries and fears, we enable ourselves to break through and invite the possibilities into our life. It doesn't have to be a birthday or a holiday to give a gift. A time when you want to share love is a time for all seasons.

A gift can be simple, extravagant, handmade or purchased in the finest store. The loving thought surrounding the act of giving is a nutrient for the spirit of the one who gives. If your gift is your time, that is sharing your most precious asset. No amount of monetary award will replace how you spend your time. Generosity and thoughtfulness will reap its own rewards. A giving person is one who appeals to all.

PLAN A DATE WITH YOUR MAN

Why wait? You have a wonderful imagination and are probably an incurable romantic. Think of the most romantic thing you would like your man to do for you and then go ahead and do it for him. In fact, do it for yourself. You'll enjoy a romantic escape.

The date you will plan can be anything you desire, from a picnic to the theater to a candlelight dinner for two in your favorite restaurant. You can even surprise him and let him think you are doing something else, when low and behold you come upon your secretly planned interlude. Think about the details and have roses for him if you like, a little card or a boutonniere. If you are going somewhere outdoors and can bring along your own music to create the mood, go ahead. The moment is yours to experience and one that you and your love will surely cherish. Creating memories is the essence of living. It is what we remember as the years go by...all the wonderful times when we share laughter, joy and love.

TAKE A RIDE ON A MERRY-GO-ROUND

Go to a nearby amusement park or plan a visit to the next fair and jump on your favorite, brightly-colored, magical horse atop a wonderful merry-go-round. Close your eyes and feel the air brush against your skin as the horse bounces up and down to the circular motion of the carousel. Remember the first time you took a ride on a merry-go-round. It seemed so large, so colorful and exciting. Rekindle the imagination and wonder of the joy of riding atop a dazzling mount on a fun-filled merry-go-round.

The feeling of freedom and joy is exciting. And feeling exciting, open to the possibilities, is definitely sexy!

TAKE A WALK THROUGH A TOY STORE

Feeling young is sexy. The joy in a child's eyes as she plays with a brand new doll. The laughter at the sight and sounds of a bright, musical toy that lights up. The giggles at the fascinating newness of a big, bouncing ball. These kinds of fresh, joyful emotions bring out the best in us. While as adults we may feel as though we have seen plenty of dolls, balls and toys, we are capable of igniting the passionate joy of a child in all that we do today.

Take a walk through a neighborhood toy store. Marvel at the detail and beauty of the porcelain dolls, the plushness of the stuffed animals and the creativity in playing some of the more exciting electronic games. Be a kid for a day. Feeling this youthfulness is sexy. A smile says it all.

SIT BY THE FIREPLACE AND DREAM

Without hope we are lost. Dreams give us the vision, the hope to continue in our quest for what we want out of life. We can never be too satisfied, for we must keep growing and challenging ourselves to greater heights. What is your dream? Sitting by a warm, cozy fireplace, looking into the crackling flames, feeling its warmth, imagine all that you want. Whatever you want out of life, envision it, see it and dream how you'll feel as your dreams become reality. Lose yourself in the dream. Take it wherever it will lead you.

ELIMINATE THE WORD "CAN'T"

If you feel you can accomplish anything, that you can realize your goals, that your dreams can become reality, you empower yourself. Feeling confident and sure of yourself is sexy. You can do it. It's an attitude. Like a fine athlete, you hone your concentration and mental energy on the positive. A "can do" attitude is energizing and exciting for others to be around. Exciting is sexy. And being sexy is exciting.

I CAN'T
I CAN'T
I CAN'T

SOME FINAL THOUGHTS ON A SEXIER YOU

Sexy is a sexy does. It is an attitude, how we feel about ourselves. Feeling sexy is about letting go of the notion that we have to be perfect. It is time to create our own personal definition of sexy as we love our body, ignite our senses, invigorate our mind and unleash our creativity. Try the plan for four weeks. You'll be surprised at the results! Feeling sexy is magnetic. We attract people to us. We are open, fun, vulnerable, exciting. Life is for the living. Try putting on a new attitude—provocative, tempting, passionate. Hug. Touch. Kiss. Squeeze the juice out of life. When we embrace the magic around us, we are able to show the world how uniquely beautiful we are. Make a wish and it will come true.

ABOUT THE AUTHOR

Paula Peisner Coxe was born and educated in Los Angeles. She was educated at the University of California, Los Angeles and completed a Master's Degree in Business Administration at the University of Southern California. Ms. Coxe is a management consultant and the author of *Finding Time: Breathing Space for Women Who Do Too Much, Finding Peace: Letting Go and Liking It,* and *Finding Love: Let Your Heart Be Your Guide.* She is currently Regional Director of a counseling service in the Northwest. Paula lives and writes in Oregon with her husband and two daughters.

 NOTES:

 NOTES:

_____

_____

_____

_____

_____

_____

_____

_____

_____

_____

_____

_____

_____

_____

_____

_____

NOTES:

_____

_____

_____

_____

_____

_____

_____

_____

_____

_____

_____

_____

_____

_____

Don't Miss
1001 Beauty Solutions
The Ultimate One-Step Adviser for Your Everyday Beauty Problems

by Beth Barrick-Hickey

- *What shampoo is best for color treated hair?*
- *Should I apply body creams in the morning or at night?*
- *How can I revive my hair style at the end of the day?*

Have your questions answered by the beauty experts at Revlon, Clairol, L'Oreal, Helene Curtis, and other world-class professionals! To bring you **1001 Beauty Solutions**, author Beth Barrick-Hickey discovered the world's most frequently asked beauty questions, and had them answered by the leading beauty specialists, salon professionals, and product manufacturers.

Building on the accomplishments of its bestselling predecessor, *500 Beauty Solutions*, **1001 Beauty Solutions** is packed with even more advice for taking care of your hair and nails and buying the lotions, potions, and products that line store shelves.

Here's what they said about *500 Beauty Solutions*:

"…a real source of information from the elementary to the more complex questions women have…it's a MUST HAVE for help."
— Linda Moran Evans, Beauty Ed., *Family Circle*

"Never has so much beauty information been compiled into one publication."
— Jacklyn Monk, Beauty Ed., *Bridal Guide*

"…takes the guesswork out of shopping for hair and nail products."
— *The Dallas Morning News*

160 pages, ISBN: 1-57071-049-X (paperback) $12.95

1001 Beauty Solutions is available now at your local bookstore.

Don't Miss These Books by Paula Peisner Coxe

Finding Time: Breathing Space for Women Who Do Too Much

Learn to successfully manage time and outside demands to find the time to enjoy life more. For every woman too tired, too busy, or just too stressed to think of herself, this bestselling book shows you how to find or make time for yourself.

256 pages, ISBN: 0-942061-33-0 (paperback) $7.95

Breathing Space: A Journal for Women Who Do Too Much

Let this elegant journal be the place where you find the peaceful time you deserve. This personal memoir is designed to breathe space into the lives of busy women across the country. Filled with quotes, inspirational suggestions, and tips from *Finding Time*, *Breathing Space* reminds you that time to yourself is important. Celebrate it within the serene pages of this beautiful journal.

160 pages, ISBN: 1-57071-036-8 (paperback) $7.95

Finding Peace: Letting Go and Liking It

Filled with carefully crafted thoughts, suggestions, and uplifting quotes to give you the opportunity to reassess how to live your life, to contemplate, to forgive and accept. Learn the secrets of letting go and liking it.

256 pages, ISBN: 1-57071-014-7 (paperback) $7.95

Finding Love: Let Your Heart Be Your Guide

Love is the greatest gift of the human heart. But how can we discover the love within us and make it a part of our everyday lives? Filled with inspirational thoughts, teachings and words of wisdom, *Finding Love* will direct you on your journey to a loving, passionate life.

288 pages, ISBN: 1-57071-031-7 (paperback) $7.95

These books by Paula Peisner Coxe are available at your local book or gift store. Call or write to Sourcebooks for a complete catalog:

Sourcebooks Inc.
P. O. Box 372
Naperville, IL 60566
(708) 961-3900
FAX: (708) 961-2168